THE LIGHT PRINCESS

A one-act dramedy by
Emily C. A. Snyder

Based on the fairy tale by George MacDonald

www.youthplays.com
info@youthplays.com
424-703-5315

 ISBN 978-1-62088-722-6.

COPYRIGHT RULES TO REMEMBER

1. To produce this play, you must receive prior written permission from YouthPLAYS and pay the required royalty.

2. You must pay a royalty each time the play is performed in the presence of audience members outside of the cast and crew. Royalties are due whether or not admission is charged, whether or not the play is presented for profit, for charity or for educational purposes, or whether or not anyone associated with the production is being paid.

3. No changes, including cuts or additions, are permitted to the script without written prior permission from YouthPLAYS.

4. Do not copy this book or any part of it without written permission from YouthPLAYS.

5. Credit to the author and YouthPLAYS is required on all programs and other promotional items associated with this play's performance.

When you pay royalties, you are recognizing the hard work that went into creating the play and making a statement that a play is something of value. We think this is important, and we hope that everyone will do the right thing, thus allowing playwrights to generate income and continue to create wonderful new works for the stage.

Plays are owned by the playwrights who wrote them. Violating a playwright's copyright is a very serious matter and violates both United States and international copyright law. Infringement is punishable by actual damages and attorneys' fees, statutory damages of up to $150,000 per incident, and even possible criminal sanctions. **Infringement is theft. Don't do it.**

Have a question about copyright? Please contact us by email at info@youthplays.com or by phone at 424-703-5315. When in doubt, please ask.

CAST OF CHARACTERS

NARRATOR, our guide through the story.

KING, the Light Princess' father.

QUEEN, the Light Princess' mother.

PRINCESS, the Light Princess.

PRINCE, falls in love with The Light Princess.

WITCH, the King's evil sister.

PRIEST, may be played by the Narrator.

NURSE, may be played by the Princess.

SERVANTS, may be played by the Narrator and the Prince.

SHEEP, may be played by the Prince.

HUM-DRUM, a Metaphysician. May be played by the Narrator.

KOPY-KECK, a Metaphysician. May be played by the Narrator.

SETTING

While this is a fairy tale, it may be set in any time or place you desire, according to your interpretation, audience, budgetary constraints and other considerations.

PRODUCTION NOTES

This adaptation of *The Light Princess* was originally intended as Theatre for Young Audiences. It has enjoyed tours, short play festivals, and full productions, and is meant to be as variable as your company requires.

In regard to staging the magical elements, companies are encouraged to discover practical or mechanical solutions as may please them. However, it should be kept in mind that low-budget, inventive solutions—puppets, balloons, silks, acrobatics, etc.—can delight just as readily as huge mechanical devices or tanks of water. The suggestions in the stage directions will be aimed towards companies with a moderate budget, but should not be taken as proscriptive in any sense.

All characters should be played as their respective ages and genders, regardless of who plays them. The Narrator may be played by an actor of any gender and should be referred to by the actor's actual sex.

Casting directors are highly encouraged to cast a diverse net in regard to sex, ethnicity, age, size, shape, ability and orientation.

Once again, especially in regard to the Prince and Princess, it is more important to cast actors of feeling and vulnerability than to cast for some absurd "beauty." Rather, cast for talent and actors capable of meeting the physical demands of your production.

Companies have permission to double and triple cast roles, or to cast separate actors in either non-speaking roles, or in small parts such as the Priest and the Metaphysicians. In that case, the Priest should be played as male, while the Metaphysicians can be played by an actor of any gender and should be referred to by the actor's own gender.

There are many long stretches indicated in the script which may be played against music, ambient noises, or silence. These sections (swimming, flying, fighting, etc.) may be whatever length the companies prefer. The importance is to achieve the effect of magic for the audience, and to let the audience have a moment to enjoy it.

In regard to the music, companies are free to compose,

commission, or pay for rights to existing music as best pleases them. The original production used original compositions by Taylor Benson that are available via iTunes and Spotify.

There are also several sections meant to be improvisational, such as the Prince's searching for a bride through the audience, and the Narrator's "game show." Treat these as bits to be added, subtracted, expanded or altered as will most please your audience and fit your own needs.

In general, the cast is welcome to improvise throughout the play as suits them, provided it does not come at the expense of the lines as written.

ACKNOWLEDGMENT

The original production of ***The Light Princess*** was presented by the Hudson Drama Society, Hudson, MA—Touring 2011-2012, with the following team:

Narrator.......................................Jeremy Saunders
King.......................................Joshua Teixeira
Queen.......................................Brooke Liebowitz
Princess.......................................Alyssa Russell
Prince.......................................Brandon Barney
Witch.......................................Sydney Orason
Princess Flier.......................................Erik Karlson
Princess Flier.......................................Brian Matthews
Princess Flier.......................................Teddy Waszazak
Director: Emily C. A. Snyder; Stage Manager/Tour Manager: Laura Fagan; Assistant Stage Managers: Monica Jean & John McLean; Costumes/Make-Up: Evelyn Page & Sadie Tremblay Hair: Steven Pena; Props: Olivia Mitchell; Lights: Kennedy Prashaw; Original Music: Taylor Benson

DEDICATION

In memory of Anne Rita Mackie Enright Gustin
Better known as Grammy
Who first bought me a notebook and told me I should write
Requiescat in Pace

SCENE 1

(The stage is set. The KING, QUEEN, PRINCE and PRINCESS are dispersed throughout the audience, silent and immobile as pictures in a book. Only the NARRATOR is on stage – and he is hiding. Note: You may wish to keep the entire company onstage for the duration of the play, or just waiting in the wings, in order to quicken entrances and exits.)

(Music. Noise. A rumble or a change of lights. The actors stir, and:)

ALL: Once upon a time!

NARRATOR: So long ago that I have quite forgotten the date, there lived a –

KING: King!

NARRATOR: And a –

QUEEN: Queen!

PRINCE: Who had no children.

(It may seem strange to have the Prince and Princess narrate when they aren't in the story yet. This device works best if the Prince and the Princess invest their lines with the fullness of their adult attraction and argumentative opinion for one another, as if they were in scene looking back on themselves.)

ALL: Awww.

PRINCESS: And the King said to himself:

KING: All the Kings of my acquaintance have children – some three, some seven, and some as many as twelve – and my Queen has not one. *(Aside:)* I begin to feel put-out.

PRINCE: So he made up his mind to be cross with his wife about it.

PRINCESS: But she bore it all like the good, patient Queen that she was.

(A rustling. The King and Queen are in scene.)

KING: Why don't you have any daughters, at least? I don't say sons; that might be too much to expect.

QUEEN: I'm sure, dear George, I'm sorry. But you must learn to have some patience.

KING: Patience? *Patience,* Penelope?! It would be one thing if we were peasants, dear, but *this* is an affair of state!

QUEEN: Ah, well, then you better have the committee look into it. *(To the audience:)* I'm sure *someone* knows how to get a little baby!

(The Narrator lifts his hand. Before anyone in the audience can answer:)

KING: No no no! Don't ask them! They might answer you! No. I see you're right, my love. We shall simply have to wait.

(They wait.)

(The Narrator enters with a baby, which he gives to the Queen, saying:)

NARRATOR: It was more than he deserved, therefore, when, at last, the Queen gave him a daughter—

PRINCE: —as lovely a little Princess—

PRINCESS: —as never, *ever* cried.

(Music. A bubble of laughter from the baby. The King and Queen look at each other in amazement, then hold the baby up, up, up. More laughter and then a hiccup. A smell. And a gurgle from the baby, as the King and Queen hold their noses. Gratefully, the Queen gives the baby to the Narrator to change her diaper as…)

SCENE 2

KING: Queen!

NARRATOR: Said the King.

KING: Our daughter must be christened!

QUEEN: So she must.

NARRATOR: Said the Queen.

QUEEN: But you must make sure, my darling George, that *someone* is forgotten.

KING: What do you mean?

QUEEN: You must *remember* to *forget.*

KING: I don't follow.

QUEEN: It's a royal christening—

KING: Of course it is! We're Kingly!

QUEEN: Which means you must remember to invite *(To the audience:)* every single person!

KING: Naturally, naturally. Unless they misbehave.

QUEEN: But you must *also* remember—

KING: What's that? I've already forgotten.

QUEEN: No, no, dear George. What I mean is... *(To the Narrator:)* Oh, do help me.

NARRATOR: *(Passing off the baby:)* What the Queen meant to say is that it was important to *remember* to forget. This might sound strange, but consider: who did the parents of Sleeping Beauty forget to invite?

(If the Narrator speaks to the audience and gets a response, then feel free to improvise a little with the audience rather than sticking rigidly to the text.)

Why they forgot their own worst enemy! The worst fairy of them all. And as a result, that fairy came and cursed everyone to sleep for a hundred years inside a silent castle.

QUEEN: *(Yawning, walking with the baby:)* I think that was a blessing.

NARRATOR: *Anyway,* when the Queen said:

QUEEN: *(Like the first time:)* "You must remember to forget!"

NARRATOR: What she *meant* was they should probably remember to forget her Great Aunt Ermengarde, who was very nice, and usually only cursed a child with a love for chocolate chip cookies.

(Producing one and munching.)

Which is really no curse at all. And one that I think most of you were cursed with.

(He may give a cookie away.)

QUEEN: Great Aunt Ermengarde gets around.

NARRATOR: So when the Queen said:

QUEEN: "You must remember to forget!"

NARRATOR: And the King said:

KING: "What's that? I've already forgotten."

NARRATOR: Both of them thought they meant the same thing. But what the Queen meant was:

QUEEN: Ask my Great Aunt Ermengarde to curse the Princess with a love of chocolate chip cookies.

(Exits with the baby.)

NARRATOR: While what the *King* meant was... What the King *meant*... What the King meant to *say* was...!

KING: "What's that? I've already forgotten."

NARRATOR: Which is a dangerous thing in a king: never to *remember,* and always to forget. For if the King *actually* forgot, why then he might have forgotten his sister. Which is bad. Because his sister is actually…*a witch.*

SCENE 3

(Lights change, dim, go strange, as the WITCH *appears.)*

WITCH: And she should *not* have been forgotten!

(Music plays, whirls, as the Witch may lightly terrorize the other actors, scatter puppet mice, steal cookies or sneer at the audience. From the shadows, the Princess bravely answers.)

PRINCESS: She was a sour, spiteful creature.

PRINCE: The wrinkles of contempt crossed the wrinkles of peevishness.

PRINCESS: And made her face as full of wrinkles as a pat of butter.

KING: If ever a king could be justified in forgetting anybody, this king was justified in forgetting…in forgetting…in forgetting…

WITCH: YOUR SISTER!

KING: Even at a christening.

PRINCESS: She looked very odd, too. Her forehead was as large as all the rest of her face, and projected over it like a precipice. When she was angry, her little eyes flashed a stormy blue.

(The Witch's eyes flash blue, red, etc. Change these colors to match whatever trick you have on hand. Teeny flashlights work.)

KING: When she hated anybody, they shone red.

PRINCE: What they looked like when she loved anybody? No one ever knew.

PRINCESS: For I never heard of her loving anybody other than herself.

NARRATOR: And she couldn't love herself at all. Now you may be inclined to feel sorry for the Witch, because although she was very clever, she:

WITCH: Never got to be the Queen!

(The Witch starts making sad faces at the audience. If she spies anyone wearing a headband or tiara, she might make a motion for it.)

NARRATOR: But what you must *remember*, is that the Witch had no compassion for anybody else. And anyone who thinks only of themselves is a very bad ruler indeed.

WITCH: AAAAAAAAAAH!

NARRATOR: In fact, the Witch did not know *how* to be happy. And so she hated anyone who was, and looked for ways to make everyone around her as miserable as herself.

(Shaking his head.)

I cannot think of anything worse than someone who hates other people's happiness.

(To the Witch:)

Hatred is like a stone that grows within your soul. Curve your life around it, and it will sink you to your grave.

(He exits to become the PRIEST.)

SCENE 4

(The Princess enters as a NURSE, carrying the "baby," who might be played by a helium balloon in a blanket. At any rate, there's a trick that isn't obvious yet. She takes up the narration:)

PRINCESS: Now when the Witch was not invited to the christening—

QUEEN: Because the King forgot to remember to forget!

PRINCESS: She did not sulk like other witches do, but she made up her mind to go anyway.

WITCH: And make the whole family *miserable.*

PRINCESS: Like the princess that she was. So she put on her best gown, and her little golden slippers, combed her hair and brushed her teeth, and went to the great palace in a carriage drawn by sheep.

(No need to go nuts, costume designers! Change "golden" as you find fancy footwear.)

PRINCE: Baaa.

PRINCESS: When she arrived, she even kissed her brother—

KING: Who forgot he had forgotten her.

PRINCESS: And took her place in the procession—making sure that she stood very near the water.

(Music, as the Narrator dressed as a Priest takes the baby and dips her in the water three times. The christening takes place sotto voce as the music rises, and the Witch sings an incantation:)

PRIEST: What name do you give your child?

WITCH: LIGHT OF SPIRIT,
BY MY CHARMS
LIGHT OF BODY,
EVERY PART

QUEEN: Lilian.

NEVER WEARY
HUMAN ARMS,
ONLY CRUSH
THY PARENTS' HEART!

PRIEST: Then I baptize you, Lilian.

LIGHT OF SPIRIT,
BY MY CHARMS,
LIGHT OF BODY,
EVERY PART

In nomine Patris, et Filii, et Spiritu Sancti.
Amen.

NEVER WEARY
HUMAN ARMS,
ONLY CRUSH
THY PARENTS' HEART

(A thunderclap. The spell takes effect. The blanket falls away from the baby, and she floats up to the ceiling. Everyone gasps and steps back, scattering in their confusion.)

(The Narrator's Priest garments fall away as he returns to himself, and looks dangerously at the Witch, who saunters off. Then to us:)

NARRATOR: The Witch removed her gravity.

SCENE 5

(The King and Queen storm on, while the Prince and the Narrator, dressed as SERVANTS, may get a ladder or some other device to coax the balloon-baby from the ceiling.)

KING: This should not have happened!

QUEEN: You should have remembered who you forgot!

KING: If I remembered, I would not have forgotten!

(The Queen bursts into tears. The King pats her awkwardly.)

I should have remembered to forget.

QUEEN: Yes.

KING: Perhaps the effect is temporary?

QUEEN: Did you ever float around when you were a child?

KING: Once. When I made my sister angry. She said I was full of "hot air," and then I was. She made a lot of puns. I hate them.

QUEEN: How did you escape her curse?

KING: Well, my dear, I farted.

(The Queen laughs helplessly, and leans back into his arm. Behind them, the Prince and Narrator, still acting as servants, do their best to get the balloon baby. They may actually be coaxing down silks for a future flying scene, or what you will. It's comical.)

NARRATOR: Careful there, careful!

PRINCE: *(Whistling:)* Here, Princess! Here, Princess! Here, Princy-poo!

(From the rafters, the sound of the infant princess laughing as she eludes them.)

KING: *(Looking thoughtfully at the Prince:)* What will she do if she's married?

QUEEN: *(Somewhat hysterically through her tears:)* She'll fill the country with bouncing baby boys!

WITCH: *(Appearing to give a drum riff:)* Ba-dum-bum-chh!

QUEEN: *(Really getting into it:)* And if she ever gets angry, she'll simply *fly off the handle!*

WITCH: *(Appearing:)* Ba-dum-bum-chh!

KING: Penelope, please!

QUEEN: *(Ignoring him—yelling at the Witch, who watches from one side:)* One thing is for certain, though.

KING: What's that?

QUEEN: At least *our* little girl will always be happy.

WITCH: Why?

QUEEN: Because nothing can get her down!

(The Queen pulls a string attached to the balloon, and the Prince and the Narrator pull apart as the baby balloon lands safely in her mother's arms.)

(The Witch scowls and exits.)

KING: *(With a pained expression:)* Please, my dear. No puns. There are a great many evils in this world, and the worst of all is punning. But if you like, I shall apologize and try to make amends.

QUEEN: It won't change a bit of her.

KING: *(Thoughtfully:)* No. But it might change a bit of me.

NARRATOR: So the King went off to see his sister to beg her to remove the curse.

KING: Sister!

NARRATOR: Cried the King.

KING: You've made your point. What do you want to remove the curse? I've tried to make the Princess fart, but she just flew around the roof like a balloon! Please. I'm begging you. I've got money.

WITCH: Eh.

KING: I'll give you…your own castle!

WITCH: Eh.

KING: I'll—I'll even make you Queen! Just, please, remove the curse!

NARRATOR: But she declared with a grave face that she:

WITCH: Knew nothing about it at all!

(The King exits despondently.)

NARRATOR: Her eyes, however, shone pink, which they only did when she made someone else unhappy.

WITCH: Which is all I ever really wanted in the first place.

(The Witch goes off cackling to herself.)

SCENE 6

NARRATOR: That was the situation above-stairs, but below-stairs it was quite different. For, if it was not easy for the Princess' nurses to hold her, at least she never made their arms ache.

(The Prince, still dressed as a Servant races on, keeping the baby balloon aloft.)

PRINCE: And she was so nice to play at ball with! There was positively no danger of letting her fall. They might throw her down—

WITCH: *(Joining in:)* Or knock her down—

NARRATOR: *(Stopping the Witch:)* Or put her down—

PRINCE: But they couldn't *let* her down.

(He runs off cradling the balloon baby.)

NARRATOR: As for the court metaphysicians,

(Revealing the puppets:)

Kopy-Keck and Hum-Drum, they said:

(The Metaphysicians can be played by separate actors, or by the Narrator using puppets. KOPY-KECK and HUM-DRUM should be wildly different—like surfer-dude vs. hyperactive dog. Feel free to change the lines slightly to fit their personalities.)

(As Hum-Drum:)

She does not belong by rights to this world at all, but to some other planet.

(As Kopy-Keck:)

Probably Mercury.

(They both laugh like pleased, wheezy Muppets, and take a bow for their nonexistent joke, but are interrupted by the Witch storming on and grabbing both puppets sternly.)

WITCH: No, no, no no no NO! Listen to me: the motion of her heart has been reversed.

NARRATOR: *(As himself:)* Reversed? And what exactly does *that* mean?

WITCH: It means, the girl's like me. It means she cannot feel. It means that I have blessed her. It means she'll never cry.

NARRATOR: And how can she be cured?

WITCH: She can't. Unless the water gets inside her. And *that*—will never happen.

(The Witch flounces off.)

SCENE 7

NARRATOR: Meantime, the Light Princess laughed and grew and floated and flew!

(A burst of music as the Light Princess herself appears, floating and laughing, dancing on air. She may fly on silks, or via harness, or swinging across the stage in the center of a cyr wheel, or doing acrobatics through the arms of other actors – whatever pleases the company.)

(It is magic. And it lingers. As does her laughter: maniacal, infectious, untamed.)

(When at last the Princess bobs to a stop, she declares:)

PRINCESS: And she never, *ever* cried!

NARRATOR: For since she had been cursed at her baptism, not a drop of water had gotten in her. And since she never touched the ground, she very rarely needed bathing. In fact, she preferred milk to water, too, and she always stayed inside the few times that it rained—laughing at the droplets and getting lost against the ceiling.

QUEEN: She could hear the most terrible things—

KING: And still the girl would laugh!

NARRATOR: The Witch's cruelty had gotten inside her. The worse something was, the more it delighted her. So, when her father told her as an experiment:

KING: The General's been cut to pieces, and all the troops are dead.

(If the company has a political bent, or would prefer to make topical statements about the new Vice Principal, you're welcome to choose three dire warnings that will delight or intrigue your audience. Otherwise, these three work just fine.)

(The Princess laughs.)

The enemy's marching to besiege our castle!

(The Princess laughter grows.)

QUEEN: We shall all die!

(The Princess howls with laughter.)

PRINCESS: What queer faces Mamma makes! And she squeezes water out of her cheeks? Funny Mamma!

KING: Your mother is *not* funny!

QUEEN: Oh, George!

KING: But if she can't feel for the country, Penelope, how can she ever rule?

PRINCESS: Do you know what I should like, Papa? To tie a string to me and fly me like a kite!

KING: *(To the Queen:)* I mean look at her! *(To the Princess:)* Look at you! Will anything make you sorry for anybody else? Your mother's crying! And now I'm screaming!

QUEEN: George...

PRINCESS: Do you know sometimes what I'm feeling? Like I'm the only person in the whole, wide world.

KING: Will you listen to her? She takes everything too lightly! Her head is in the clouds! *And now I'm making puns!*

PRINCESS: Oh, look at Papa's face! It's gone all purple! How funny Papa is! Do it again!

(The King growls and tries to catch the Princess.)

NARRATOR: Round and around and around they went! The King became—

KING: So furious!

NARRATOR: That he threw his glass of water at her. When suddenly...

(The Princess bumps to the floor.)

The Princess became grounded.

WITCH: *(Appearing:)* Ba-dum-bum-chhh.

(The King groans at the pun.)

NARRATOR: The King sent for his court Metaphysicians, *(Whipping out the puppets again:)* who said—

QUEEN: *(Silencing the puppets:)* If water will help the Princess' gravity, she should be *made* to cry.

KING: What? Shall I whip her?

WITCH: *(Whispering in the King's ear:)* Strike her!

(The Witch raises the King's hand, but the Princess, although frightened, begins to laugh. Everyone is taken aback, even the Witch.)

KING: And still the Princess laughs!

QUEEN: Although it sounds like screaming.

NARRATOR: Perhaps the best thing for the Princess would have been to fall in love.

QUEEN: But how a Princess who has no gravity could fall into *anything* is a difficulty—

KING: Perhaps *the* difficulty. Unless...

QUEEN: *(Clapping her hands:)* The lake!

KING: *(Bringing out the lake:)* Yes! If water makes her grave—

WITCH: Then the Princess should be laid in one.

(The King and Queen make a lake with lengths of cloth, ribbons, lights, or wood, while the Witch recoils, leaving the Princess to contemplate the water "alone.")

PRINCESS: But there remained the difficulty of how she should get *in* the lake. For she had as great a fear of the open air as most children have of the sea. If an errant wind should catch me, I would float away forever...! What I need—

NARRATOR: Thought she.

PRINCESS: Is someone who can *make* me fall.

SCENE 8

(With a fanfare, the Prince enters, possibly riding a horse—possibly riding a horse à la Monty Python; certainly behaving as pompously and "princely" as possible. The mood is altered. This is something different.)

PRINCE: It must have been about this time that the son of a king, who lived a thousand miles away, set out to look for the daughter of a queen.

(Moving through the audience:)

He travelled far and wide, but as soon as he found a princess, he found some fault in her.

(The Prince spends some time improvising through the audience. This period can be as long or as short as preferred. Each person he approaches should be considered and rejected—although kindly. So, nothing like: "You're old and ugly," but things like: "Not you; you're my Dad" are fine.)

(It also always gets a laugh to have the Prince reject someone for his or her good qualities. "Too pretty," is generally good. "Too tall," to any infants in the audience. Well known audience members might get a little fun poked at them. Even there, be gentle.)

(Once it's clear he's done with the audience—typically some agreed-upon rejection, the Narrator interrupts with:)

NARRATOR: Of course, he could not marry a mere woman, however beautiful; and there were No Other Princesses to be found worthy of him.

PRINCESS: Whether the Prince was so near perfection that he had a right to demand perfection itself, I cannot pretend to say. All I know is that he was a—

PRINCE: Fine, handsome, brave, generous, well-bred, and well-behaved youth, as all princes are.

PRINCESS: In his wanderings, he had come across some reports about our princess.

PRINCE: But as everybody said she was –

NARRATOR: *(Running across, or otherwise popping up:)* BEWITCHED!

PRINCE: He never dreamed that *she* could bewitch him.

(The Prince might go up to where the Princess floats in her castle made of air, and play with her; poking her; prodding her; dribbling her up and down, swinging her cyr wheel or tugging on her silks.)

For what indeed could a prince do with a princess that had lost her gravity? Who could tell what she might lose next? She might lose her visibility, or her tangibility; or, in short, the power of making impressions. He did not think of her again.

PRINCESS: *(Furious:)* Then one day, he lost sight of his retinue in a great forest!

(A forest appears. Any attendants disperse. Perhaps the Princess rains down leaves upon him, perhaps the others come on with branches, or maybe just the Narrator and others stand in his way with sticks tangled behind his head.)

(Either way, the Prince accepts his location philosophically and addresses the audience.)

PRINCE: These forests are very useful; they help the princes get away to follow their fortunes. In this way princes have the advantage over princesses, who are forced to marry before they have had a bit of fun. I wish our princesses got lost in the forest sometimes.

(The Prince sighs and shakes himself out of his ruminations. The Princess is rather touched, and has all but forgotten her anger. If it could be said she is following him through the air, she is

following him. The forests rustle and part to reveal the lake again. It is night.)

One lovely evening, after wandering about for many days, he found himself by the side of the lake. Suddenly he paused, and listened. Strange sounds came across the water.

(Silence. The Princess has been listening to his story. The Prince sighs and:)

I *said*: "Strange sounds came across the water."

PRINCESS: Oh!

(She plunges into the water with a delighted shriek.)

PRINCE: It was, in fact, the Princess laughing.

NARRATOR: Now there was something odd in her laugh, something missing. Something like…

PRINCE: The possibility of sorrow.

(The Prince strips off his outer layer, as the Narrator speaks.)

NARRATOR: And this was how the Prince mistook the laughter for screaming. He saw something white in the water. He plunged in.

(Let this white refer to clothing, not skin.)

SCENE 9

(The Prince dives into the water, completely submerged beneath the waves. The Narrator glances over from his perch.)

NARRATOR: He soon reached the white object, and found that it was—

PRINCE: *(Rising from the water with a gasp:)* A woman!

(He dives back in.)

NARRATOR: There was not light enough to show that she was in fact—

PRINCESS: *(Also surfacing to shake off the Prince:)* A Princess!

(She is pulled under.)

NARRATOR: But quite enough to show that she was a lady, for it does not want much light to see that. Round and around they went, he trying to catch her leg while she kicked him away, so that you never saw so reluctant a rescuer topple out of the lake.

(The Prince and the Princess topple out. Perhaps the lake gives way before them. The Prince has the Princess about the waist. There may be seaweed in her hair.)

(For a moment, she lies gasping on the ground, trying to speak as she rolls over to face him. They are silent, seeing each other for the first time. Until, suddenly, the Princess is caught up by the wind and screeches:)

PRINCESS: You naughty, naughty, NAUGHTY, NAUGHTY man!

PRINCE: What?

PRINCESS: I'll tell Papa.

PRINCE: *(Trying to catch her foot:)* Oh no, you won't!

PRINCESS: Yes, I will. What business had you to pull me down out of the water, and throw me to the bottom of the air? I never did you any harm.

PRINCE: Pardon me. I did not mean to hurt you.

PRINCESS: I don't believe you have any brains; and that is a worse loss than your wretched gravity. I pity you.

(The Prince bursts out laughing. Offended, the Princess stomps her foot and nearly flies away, but catches hold of the Prince's sleeve.)

Put me up directly.

PRINCE: Put you up where, you beauty?

NARRATOR: He had fallen in love with her almost, already. For her anger made her more charming than before; and, as far as he could see, which certainly was not far, she had not a single fault about her. Except, of course, that she had no gravity. No prince, however, would judge a princess by her weight.

PRINCE: Put you up where, you beauty?

PRINCESS: In the water, you stupid!

PRINCE: How am I to put you in?

PRINCESS: That is your business. You took me out—put me in again.

PRINCE: Very well.

NARRATOR: Said the Prince; and, catching her up in his arms, he sprang with her from the rock. The Princess had just time to give one delighted shriek of laughter before the water closed over them again. They swam.

(They dive in again—but perhaps this time, we can see them as they go. It may be more dance than backstroke, perhaps backlit behind a curtain, perhaps once more with seaweed silks and scrim. The Narrator may calmly blow bubbles to emulate a passing fish. Music. [There are lyrics from George MacDonald in the original novella for the Prince here, if you want to compose a song with his text. They're at the beginning of Chapter 10.])

(There is much beauty in it. It's a little like flying. It's slipping and catching and gliding away again. The Prince may almost steal a kiss – before the Princess floats upwards to the rocks, and they stay tethered there together.)

For weeks and weeks, the Prince visited the Princess, always meeting her in the water. When she arrived, she floated down with ribbons on her waist so he could pull her under. And every night when she left him to return into the air, she'd whisper in his ear:

PRINCESS: Don't tell.

NARRATOR: She was very different in the water, although the Prince could hardly know that. There was something about the stillness of the lake that made the Princess almost peaceable. Perhaps because there's something about great pleasure that defies all laughter. You have no need to laugh, when the world is cool and calm.

(The rock. Moonlight. The seaweed is brushed out of the Princess' hair. The Prince looks at her, besotted. Then:)

PRINCE: How do you like falling in?

PRINCESS: Is that what you call *falling in*? It seems to me like going up.

(The Prince grins.)

How do YOU like falling in?

(The Prince captures her lips with his own.)

(She disengages, saying:)

No more of that: I am tired of it. I must go home.

(She swims to one side.)

PRINCE: Will you be in the lake tomorrow night?

PRINCESS: To be sure I will. I don't think so. Perhaps. Good night, Prince.

PRINCE: How do you know I am a prince, Princess?

PRINCESS: Because you are a very nice young man, Prince.

PRINCE: Do you love me, Princess?

(The Princess laughs.)

I'm being serious. Do you love me?

PRINCESS: Yes. Why not? Help me fall in.

(The Prince and Princess recede beneath the waves.)

SCENE 10

NARRATOR: When the King's sister learnt how the lake affected the Princess, she flew into a rage. For what she chiefly hated was someone else's happiness. If the water made the Princess happy, if it made her *almost* capable of love, then her Aunt…

(The Witch appears, more fearsome than before.)

WITCH: Would drain the water dry.
So that even babies couldn't cry.
And all the Kingdom will surely die,
Or be as miserable as I.

(She bares her arm and begins stirring it over the water where the lovers swim. A white serpent slithers in, over the audience's head, from the back. This, too, may be a puppet, engineered by crew members or any extra cast members. Fancy light displays also work. Whatever you do, aim for delighted shivers. The waves grow choppy, as lights stream upward to her wand. She sings, with accompaniment:)

WITCH: DEATH ALONE FROM DEATH CAN SAVE.
LOVE IS DEATH, AND SO IS BRAVE—

LOVE CAN FILL THE DEEPEST GRAVE.
LOVE LOVES ON...*BENEATH* THE WAVE.

Drink! Drink, my serpent! Drink!

(She throws a handful of fairy dust or fire into the water, just as the serpent attaches itself to the corner of the lake. The water begins to rush out into its maw.)

PRINCESS: *(Surfacing and gripping the water:)* No....

PRINCE: What is it? Are you ill?

PRINCESS: It's sinking!

PRINCE: What is?

PRINCESS: The water! I...I can't stay...!

(The Princess gets pulled away into the air. The Prince looks around for the source of the drainage, eventually sighting the serpent.)

PRINCE: *(Trying to snatch the water:)* Give it back!

(The music rises as the serpent drains all the water. The Witch continues singing, while the Narrator locates the Prince's sword and throws it to him. Louder now:)

NARRATOR: *(Throwing the sword:)* Here!	**WITCH:** DEATH ALONE FROM DEATH CAN SAVE. LOVE IS DEATH AND SO IS BRAVE
PRINCE: *(To the serpent:)* Give it back!	LOVE CAN FILL THE DEEPEST GRAVE LOVE LOVES ON BENEATH THE WAVE!

(The music continues as the Prince and serpent enter into an epic battle: the Prince nearly tugging the water out of the serpent's mouth; the serpent nipping the Prince on his arm.

Until, swooping up his sword with his good arm, the Prince skewers the serpent through the jaw.)

(The Witch shrieks as the Princess flies in, faltering a little, scrambling after the last of the water...but it is gone.)

(If she could weep, she would: but instead the Princess is reduced to horrible laughter to try to express this newfound sense of pain.)

(She is nearly grounded. She is floating very near the earth. The Witch walks around her.)

WITCH: The poor Princess nearly went out of what little mind she had. As the lake began to sink, the Princess faded to a shadow of herself.

PRINCESS: But she never, *ever* cried.

WITCH: This is not enough! May every spring that throbs and bubbles, die away like the pulse of a dying man. Let their brains boil and frizzle in their skulls!

Let no rain fall nor no one in the Kingdom cry.
Let every heart and mouth be papery and dry.
And as you laugh, sweet Princess, be as miserable as I.

(Lights down on the tableau: the Witch holding the fallen Princess' chin, while the poor girl laughs and laughs and laughs and laughs and...)

SCENE 11

NARRATOR: The Prince waited all night by the edge of the empty lake, but the Princess never came. Worried, he made up his mind to go seek her out, and promptly went to the castle.

PRINCE: *(Knocking:)* Let me in!

QUEEN: Who are you?

PRINCE: *(Quickly bowing, hiding his hurt arm:)* Pardon me, Majesty. I am a…a…shoe maker.

QUEEN: A…shoe maker?

PRINCE: A shoe maker. For the Princess.

QUEEN: Her feet rarely touch the ground. She has no need of shoes.

PRINCE: Please…I…I need…I must…I am…

QUEEN: *(Wisely:)* Come in, then. She keeps to her room, with the curtains drawn, to shut out the dying lake.

WITCH: *(Still circling the Princess:)* But she could not shut it out of her mind. It haunted her imagination, so that she felt as if the lake were her—

PRINCESS: Soul, drying up within me, first to:

PRINCESS & WITCH: Mud.

WITCH: Then to:

PRINCESS & WITCH: Madness…

PRINCESS: And then to—

WITCH: Death.

PRINCE: As for the Prince?

PRINCESS: She had forgotten him.

(The Prince reels back and sits to one side, polishing a shoe. The King storms in, followed by the Narrator, with puppets!)

NARRATOR: The King consulted his Metaphysicians!

(With all the ensuing jokes, you are more than welcome to come up with your own shtick. Just follow the rule of threes, and remember there are kids sitting in your audience. Probably.)

(As Hum-Drum:)

If the lake should disappear, the Princess will die.

(As Kopy-Keck:)

But you shall have to cremate her...for she never will be grave!

(Both puppets crack up laughing. As Hum-Drum:)

You could bury her in the evening.

(As Kopy-Keck:)

Why the evening?

(As Hum-Drum:)

Because then she won't be light!

(Both puppets laugh. The King groans. As Kopy-Keck:)

I know what will cheer her up!

(As Hum-Drum:)

What's that?

(As Kopy-Keck:)

An ice cream float!

(They both fall over themselves laughing – until they're caught in a stranglehold by the King.)

KING: Enough of that! Is there nothing to be done?

NARRATOR: *(As Hum-Drum initially, until the King pulls the puppets off:)* There is but one solution: the body –

(As himself:)

The body of a living man alone can stanch the flow. He must stand in the lake where the serpent drained it dry, and let the waters flow back in until they cover his head, and he no more can breathe. The man must give his life of his own free will; and the lake must take his life as it is filled. Elsewise the offering is of no avail. If the nation cannot provide one hero –

WITCH: Then it is time the nation should perish.

QUEEN: This was a very disheartening revelation to the King—

KING: *(Into the audience, soliciting victims:)* Not that he was unwilling to sacrifice a subject—

QUEEN: *(Stopping him:)* But that it was hopeless to find a man willing to sacrifice himself. Even for the love of a princess.

(Optional Improvisation: In performances, it was found helpful to have this little gameshow before everything becomes bleak. Companies can choose to keep or cut the following improvisation as they see fit. The purpose of including it would be to make sure that especially very young audiences knew that, ultimately, Everything Would Be All Right, and that this was Just A Play, and that no one who "drowned" was in any more danger than being covered by some material. This interaction was well received, and did not seem to take anything away from the emotional punch of the following section.)

KING: *(To the Narrator:)* Unless…?

NARRATOR: Alright! It's time to play: *WHO'S WILLING TO DROWN?* The game show where we discover who can swim and who will sink. Who'd like to come on down?

(Wheel of Drowning. Final Jeopardy. Family Funeral. *Go ahead and be as clever as you like. The Narrator goes into the audience and selects three volunteers. He should bring them up to whatever apparatus you will use for the drowning: whether that's a trapdoor on the stage or in an elevated platform, or a series of silks curtains, or wooden flats, or an actual pool of water. Whatever it is, make sure it's safe for audience members to be near.)*

(The Narrator then interacts with each audience member, asking them set questions such as:)

And what's your name? Where do you come from? *(Or:)* What school do you go to? *(Or:)* Who's your homeroom teacher?

(Then riffing momentarily off of each answer. He then concludes each mini-interview with a variation of:)

And are you willing to jump in some water today? *(Or:)* Did you bring your bathing suit? *(Or:)* How long can you hold your breath underwater?

(The Narrator then invites the volunteer to get into the apparatus – however, at the last second, he – or one of the other cast members, such as the King, Queen or Witch should object with something like:)

WITCH: No, no, no! This one's no good! They can hold their breath! *(Or:)* This person's a lifeguard! *(Or:)* They can't go in. Their mother will *kill* me!

(The more localized and specific you can get, the better. See if you can get a prominent adult to come up and maybe even get pretty far near the drowning trick – maybe ask your Principal or Mayor if you can squirt a water gun in her face. There should be a town carnival feel to it all, so that we conclude with the King chasing everyone off:)

KING: Useless! Just useless!

SCENE 12

QUEEN: No time could be lost, however, for the Princess was lying motionless on her bed.

WITCH: With no one come to rescue her. If she was even worth the effort.

(The women part to leave the Prince alone with the audience. Things have changed. He speaks simply and without artifice.)

PRINCE: She will die if I don't do it, and life would be nothing to me without her; so I shall lose nothing by doing it. And life will be as pleasant to her as ever, for she will have her lake again, and will soon forget me. And there will be so much more beauty and happiness in the world with that glorious creature diving beneath the waves! *(Beat.)* To be sure, I shall not see it. Although, perhaps, she will come visit me, or my body, stuck beneath the waves. Perhaps she will shed a tear.

(He takes a deep breath. Pushes back a sniff. Paces.)

I should leave. This country's affairs are no concern of mine. And the Princess is...is a simply heartless creature. She has already forgotten me! And to tell the truth, I love her more than she is capable of returning. If I die, she will not care. Then I should leave her and this entire land to perish...! Yet: What sort of king would run away from trouble? What sort of man am I, if I cannot feel sorry for someone else?

I will do it. *(Having made up his mind, he lets out a rather terrified laugh.)* It's rather hard to be drowned by inches, though! Let me see—that will be seventy inches *(Or however tall the actor is.)* of me to drown. *(He tries to laugh, but gets choked up.)* The longer the better, however. I will—I will bargain that the Princess stay beside me all the time. So I shall see her once more, kiss her perhaps—who knows?—and die looking in her eyes. It will be no death. At least, I shall not feel it.

You have fallen in once already—foolish Prince! You have never gotten out.

All right. I am ready.

(The Prince goes to knock on the door to the King, who is once again plagued by his Metaphysicians.)

NARRATOR: *(As Hum-Drum:)* I think it would be nice to bury her in September.

(As Kopy-Keck:)

Why September?

(As Hum-Drum:)

Because then it would be...Fall!

(They laugh and play keep-away with the King, who chases them in time to the Prince's knocking.)

KING: Go away!

(The Prince knocks again.)

It's a capital crime to knock on my door! Who is it?

PRINCE: Your butler.

KING: Buttle somewhere else. I'm busy.

PRINCE: Please, Your Majesty, I must come in! I—am not your butler.

KING: Good!

PRINCE: I'm...a shoe maker. Please let me in...if you have a soul.

KING: Is the fellow mad? Is this a pun? If it is, I'm coming to cut off your head, you rascal!

(The Metaphysicians get nervous, and run away with the Narrator. Perhaps they hide trembling behind a box or in the wings, while the King wrestles with an overlarge sword.)

Well?

(Wrenching open the door and putting his sword beneath the Prince's chin.)

What do you mean?

PRINCE: I volunteer as tribute.

(Feel free to change this if it's no longer amusing.)

NARRATOR: The King was in such a rage that before he could speak—

QUEEN: *(Rushing in to take the sword:)* He took the time to reflect that it would be a great waste to kill the only man who was willing to die.

KING: Oh! Oh! Oh, I see. Yes. That is. I am...*much obliged* to you, my young man. Take a glass of wine?

PRINCE: No, thank you.

KING: Very well. I will.

(The Queen quickly takes the wine from the King, perhaps passing it to the Narrator.)

You understand the conditions, of course.

PRINCE: I do.

KING: You will be chained in the lake, and let the water rush over your head and, uh...and...

(Making various death mimes.)

PRINCE: I understand.

KING: Excellent. Wine?

PRINCE: No, Majesty.

KING: Oh, well. More for—yes.

(The Queen divests her husband of the decanter. The Metaphysicians, however, might be getting drunk.)

Would you like to run and see your...whatchamacallit...your parents before you, er, die?

PRINCE: No, thank you.

KING: Then you're ready now?

PRINCE: I see no reason to hesitate.

KING: *(Clapping his hands:)* Excellent! Let's go at once. Her Highness is very ill.

PRINCE: But I do have one condition.

KING: What! A condition! With me! How dare you?

QUEEN: *(Overlapping:)* George—

PRINCE: You have another man willing to die? Good luck to you then!

(He starts to go:)

KING: Wait!... Yes… No… Come back! You wretch! I'll have you put in a sack, and stuck in the hole!

QUEEN: George!

PRINCE: DEATH ALONE FROM DEATH CAN SAVE.

PRINCE & QUEEN: LOVE IS DEATH, AND SO IS BRAVE—	**KING:** *(Overlapping.)* Stop that infernal racket!
PRINCE, QUEEN, NARRATOR: LOVE CAN FILL THE DEEPEST GRAVE.	I'll have 'em sew your lips shut!
LOVE LOVES ON BENEATH THE WAVE.	Guards! Guards!

KING: *(To the Queen:)* Give me back my sword! I'll make him lose his head!

QUEEN: George! George! Please! You're dangerously close to punning!

PRINCE: *(With a little bow:)* You can kill me if you like, Majesty. It will do you no good: the victim must offer himself willingly. But if you *want* your daughter to die, then by all means!

(He leaps down from his platform and opens the collar of his shirt, baring his neck.)

I am yours to command.

KING: *(After a moment:)* Well…you have offered yourself.

PRINCE: Yes, upon one condition.

QUEEN: *(Before the King can speak:)* Which is?

PRINCE: Only this: that, as I must on no account die before I am fairly drowned, and since the waiting will be rather wearisome, that the Princess, your daughter, shall go with me…feed me with her own hands, and…look at me now and then to comfort me.

(Before the King can interrupt.)

For you must confess it *is* rather hard to drown by inches. As soon as the water is up to my eyes, she may go and be happy, and forget her poor servant.

NARRATOR: Here the Prince's voice faltered, and he very nearly grew—

PRINCE: *(Quickly. Trying not to cry:)* Sentimental.

NARRATOR: In spite of his resolution.

PRINCE: Do you grant it?

KING: *(After a push from the Queen:)* Of course I do.

PRINCE: Very well. I am ready.

(He picks up his princely cape or tunic.)

NARRATOR: For he was resolved to die like a prince.

KING: A prince? He said he was my butler.

QUEEN: A shoe maker, dear.

KING: A *shoe maker? (Looking at his own worn boots:)* Not a very good one.

PRINCE: *(Reappearing in full princely regalia:)* Not *yours*, Majesty. *Hers*. The Princess—

PRINCESS: *(Appearing:)* Recognized him at once, but did not think it worthwhile to acknowledge him.

(A beat.)

PRINCE: Put me in.

SCENE 13

NARRATOR: So they did.

(Music. Very different from before. Everything is different from before. This is how the fairy tale ends.)

(The Prince is put into the hole in the lake, feet first, with a stone around his ankles. The Princess floats down to be tethered to a boat, stocked with food and wine.)

(Sunset. The distant drip of water. The King and Queen retire to one side. The Witch glides in, quite somber now as well. The Narrator perches high above, his useless puppets dangling from his belt.)

(Time passes. Someone begins blowing bubbles. More, and more, and more. A sound. A wave. The Narrator barely looks up as:)

Presently a little wave flowed over the stone, and wetted one of the Prince's knees. But he did not mind it much. He began to sing to keep his mind from drowning.

PRINCE: *(Shivering:)* DEATH ALONE
FROM DEATH CAN SAVE.
LOVE IS DEATH, AND SO IS BRAVE—
LOVE CAN FILL THE DEEPEST GRAVE.
LOVE LOVES ON BENEATH…THE…

PRINCESS: Sing again, Prince. It makes it less tedious.

NARRATOR: But the Prince was too much overcome to sing anymore; he could feel the water rising.

PRINCESS: This is very kind of you, Prince.

(She lies back in the boat, sunbathing.)

PRINCE: I am sorry I can't return the compliment.

(The Princess laughs, and one stray hand grazes the Prince's cheek.)

But you are worth dying for, after all.

(Silence. The water rises. The bubbles float. The Princess falls asleep in her boat.)

NARRATOR: Again a wavelet, and another, and another flowed over the stone, and wetted both the Prince's knees; but he did not speak or move. Two—three—four hours passed in this way, until the water brushed his elbows.

PRINCE: *(A little desperate and frightened:)* Princess! If you please—

PRINCESS: *(Sitting up:)* I'm afloat! I'm afloat!

PRINCE: Princess! If you please....

PRINCESS: *(Dragging her fingers in the water, without looking at the Prince:)* Well?

PRINCE: Well...your—your Papa promised that you would look at me, and you haven't looked at me once.

PRINCESS: *(Laughing:)* Did he? Then I suppose I must. But I am so sleepy!

PRINCE: *(Bitterly:)* Then by all means—sleep!

PRINCESS: Really, you are very good. I think I will.

PRINCE: First, though, will you give me a drink of water?

PRINCESS: *(Still not looking; rather coldly:)* When you're going to drown?

PRINCE: Some wine, then.

PRINCESS: Very well. Oh!

(Seeing him:)

Why, Prince, you don't look very well at all. Why don't you come out?

PRINCE: I dare not, Princess.

PRINCESS: *(With a giggle:)* Are you sure you don't mind it?

PRINCE: Not a bit. *(Trying not to faint as the water rises:)* I shall die before it is done, unless I have something to eat. I...dare not move. You must feed me.

PRINCESS: Did my Papa promise that, too?

PRINCE: He did. Do you mind?

PRINCESS: ...No.

(She begins feeding him bits of bread or fruit, as the water continues to rise up to the Prince's chest. Music. Water. Twilight. And:)

NARRATOR: The water flowed in nicely, now. As the Princess fed him, he contrived to kiss the tips of her fingers now and then. She did not seem to mind it, one way or the other. But the Prince felt better. Evening came, and–

PRINCESS: The moon! I had forgotten what it looked like! Let us go for a swim!

PRINCE: I shall never swim again.

PRINCESS: Oh. I forgot.

NARRATOR: The water was now up to his neck.

PRINCE: *(Almost at his last breath:)* Will you kiss me, Princess?

PRINCESS: Yes, I will.

(She leans over to kiss him.)

NARRATOR: Said she, with a kiss both sweet and cold.

PRINCE: Then I die happy.

NARRATOR: He did not speak again.

SCENE 14

(Time passes.)

QUEEN: The Princess gave him some wine for the last time: he was past eating.

(Time.)

KING: She sat down again, and looked at him. The water rose and rose.

(Time.)

QUEEN: It touched his chin.

KING: It touched his lower lip.

NARRATOR: It touched between his lips.

WITCH: He shut them hard to keep it out.

QUEEN: The Princess began to feel strange.

NARRATOR: It touched his upper lip.

KING: He breathed through his nostrils.

WITCH: The Princess looked wild.

NARRATOR: It covered his nostrils.

(He returns to blowing bubbles with perfect coldness.)

WITCH: There was fear in the Princess' face—

KING: Her eyes shone strange in the moonlight.

PRINCESS: It's covering his eyes....

QUEEN: His head fell back as the water closed over it—

WITCH: And the bubbles of his last breath bubbled up through the waves.

SCENE 15

(Silence.)

(No music. No sound. Only the quiet susurration of anyone still callous enough to blow bubbles can be heard. The Prince must be dead – he must be. The waters lap the boat and make it tip and bob. The Princess grips the sides, still looking down at the strange and submerged face.)

(She takes one breath. Whispers.)

PRINCESS: Come back.

(The creeping sound of water, calmly pouring down his lungs. She takes a second breath.)

Come back.

(Three. She laughs, hates herself for laughter, shrieks out in laughter, begins to rise into the air with the force of it, holding onto the edges of the boat by just her fingertips as her feet dangle in the air and her laughing shrieks fill the air, and:)

COME BACK!

(She dives into the water.)

(Music. Sound. The Witch springs back to life.)

(Beneath the wave, now visible, the Princess tugs at the Prince's bonds. Bobs up to breathe and sinks back beneath the wave. The King rushes forward, but is stopped by the Queen, who knows when a girl must fight things for herself.)

(The Princess thrashes against the bonds, while the Prince remains hopelessly immobile, swaying gently with the current. Above, the Witch raises her arm, and summons the white serpent

to slither into sight: its broken jaw open to swallow the lovers whole.)

(The Princess grips her Prince, and kicks the serpent. It goes wide, but circles back around. The Witch continues singing from above:)

WITCH: DEATH ALONE FROM DEATH CAN SAVE…

(The white serpent attacks, but the Princess has a plan, and, positioning the Prince's feet, she has the serpent's tooth cut the captive's bonds free.)

WITCH & QUEEN: LOVE IS DEATH AND SO IS BRAVE…

(The Princess grasps her Prince about the waist, and races for the surface, tumbling out of the water together.)

WITCH & QUEEN & KING: LOVE CAN FILL THE DEEPEST GRAVE…

PRINCESS: Help him! Help him!

(For the wind has caught the Princess, and she grasps for anything to get her down to earth. The Queen rushes forward, bending over his body and pushing back her sleeves.)

WITCH & KING & NARRATOR: LOVE LOVES ON BENEATH THE…

QUEEN: Bring him to me.

(The Queen begins resuscitation on the Prince. But with every breath she swells into his body, the Witch draws it out again. Breathe in, pound – the chest collapses, lifeless.)

(Until, gradually. Gradually. The music fades. Silence once again.)

(The Queen steps back and shakes her head. He's gone.)

SCENE 16

(The King reaches up his hand, and helps glide the Princess down. She is giggling; but still she cannot cry. The King and Queen retreat. Even the Narrator stops blowing bubbles and leaves them. The Witch remains, looming over the hovering Princess, who can't stuff the hateful laughter back into her mouth.)

WITCH: Are you happy, Princess?

(The Princess laughs against her will. Then shoves her hands against her mouth to keep the laughter in. She shakes her head.)

Good. That's all I ever wanted.

(The Witch withdraws.)

(Moonlight. Silence. The grave.)

(The very end of the world.)

(Alone, the Light Princess drags herself inch by inch towards the body of her Prince. As close as she can, she cradles his head and whispers in his lifeless ear:)

PRINCESS: Please?

(No response. But from sometime long ago and rather broken:)

LIGHT OF SPIRIT, BY MY CHARMS,
LIGHT OF BODY, EVERY PART,
NEVER WEARY HUMAN ARMS,
ONLY CRUSH YOUR LOVER'S HEART.

LIGHT OF SPIRIT, BY MY CHARMS,
LIGHT OF BODY, EVERY PART,
NEVER WEARY HUMAN ARMS,
ONLY CRUSH YOUR PRINCESS'…ONLY CRUSH…ONLY…

(She raises one cold, trembling hand to her cheek. Water. She laughs, but it comes out as a sob.)

(More water. Splashing on the Prince's cheek, and making just his fingertips stir. She laughs again: what is this from her eyes? She throws her head back to crow out laughter; it comes out as a groan.)

(Elsewhere on the stage.)

NARRATOR: *(Entering with an umbrella:)* For the first time in her life, the Princess wept. All the pent-up tears of her life poured out of her. All the water she never touched. All the water from her christening, to the water in the well, every tear she never cried coursed throughout her body, flooding through her, more than any lake or stream or cataract or thundercloud…

(A gut-wrenching sob, and the Princess drops heavily to the floor. A thunderclap, and the Narrator coolly opens his umbrella and begins to walk around. She sinks lower and lower, wringing out her heart now, while the Prince blinks, shakes his head and stirs.)

And there was rain—

QUEEN: *(Opening her umbrella:)* Such a rain!

NARRATOR: As was never seen before or since.

(The sound rises, mixing with the Princess. The Prince sits up, feels the cool water on his face, quite different from drowning in the lake. He laughs and breathes it in.)

KING: It swept away the house of her wicked, wicked Aunt!

WITCH: What? What's this? No! No! Noooooooo!

(The King might beat the Witch away with his long umbrella, as she's suddenly carried off by all the water, her white serpent following hungrily after her. Satisfied, the King pops open his umbrella, and wanders back to his Queen.)

QUEEN: It filled up every lake and pool and stream and waterfall—

PRINCE: It made such a rainbow!

NARRATOR: As was never seen before or since.

QUEEN: It made the babies cry—

KING: *(Wrapping his arm around his bride:)* It made the King cry, too.

(The King and Queen kiss behind their umbrellas, perhaps half-seen in silhouette as they might have been in younger days. They exit. Elsewhere, the Narrator closes up his umbrella and shakes it dry.)

NARRATOR: And if her laugh sounded like screaming before, now her tears sounded very much like—

PRINCE: Joy.

(The Narrator gives the Prince a little nod, and wanders off, grinning upward at the rain on his face, his umbrella over one shoulder.)

(The Princess' weeping has slowed into hiccups now—which turns into a gasp as her Prince kneels before her. She shakes her head and pulls away: it cannot be.)

(And yet it is. With a fierceness, she embraces him. When they pull away:)

PRINCESS: *(Touching her wet cheeks:)* What is this?

PRINCE: *(Collecting a tear:)* This—is sorrow, Princess.

PRINCESS: *(Still weepy:)* Then why do I feel so happy?

(The Prince laughs and offers her his hand. She takes it, stumbling against his body: she has never walked before.)

Ugh! And this, I suppose is your wretched gravity?

PRINCE: *(Sweeping her into his arms:)* No. No, Princess. This is Light.

(They kiss as the world becomes more luminous.)

(Music.)

(Rain.)

(Breath, and:)

(End of play.)

The Author Speaks

What inspired you to write this play?

I have always loved fairy tales. When I was young, I devoured Hans Christian Anderson and the Brothers Grimm. So, it wasn't long before I discovered George MacDonald! Many fairy tales invoke a sense of wonder—*The Light Princess* was perhaps one of the first that made me sob hysterically in my bed. Good sobs. Sobs that make you know you're alive. When I was working for the Hudson Drama Society, they wanted a play that they could tour: which meant no huge set, movable parts, small cast. I suggested that *The Light Princess* would fit nicely, and they gave me free rein to adapt the piece and play with the text…and to somehow make a Princess float and fly! It was an absolute delight for the whole six months the cast and crew worked together. We knew we were making something special.

Was the structure or other elements of the play influenced by any other work?

I'm a writer-director. That means that the way I "finish" writing a piece of work is I put it on its feet. In this case, I had been playing more and more with telling story through silence—weaving in and out of music and motion to text and back again. George MacDonald's story was already set up with enough fantastic elements—flying, swimming, singing—that it was fun to give the text room to breathe, to allow in that element of wonder. I'd also been working quite a bit with leaving room for improvisation from the cast. I firmly believe that theatre is best when it's crackling and alive for each particular audience. Prior to ***The Light Princess,*** I had directed ***The Taming of the Shrew*** with a lot of room for improvisation and *commedia dell'arte* influences. The audiences loved it! I think yours will, too.

Have you dealt with the same theme in other works that you have written?
Absolutely! As some wise person once said, when you're young, you hear a certain poem, and you spend the rest of your life trying to capture that poem again. For me, I often write the "smart little girl with no heart," the woman who struggles to allow herself to care. Psyche from ***Cupid and Psyche*** is like that, as is our titular Light Princess. There's a danger in vulnerability that's beautiful to dissect.

What writers have had the most profound effect on your style?
Goodness! I'd say C. S. Lewis, G. K. Chesterton and Terry Pratchett are a profound trifecta! Although they're novelists and not dramatists, there's an airy yet precise quality to their language which creeps consistently into my work. Although, truth be told, I'm a stylist. That means, my language will alter depending on the piece I'm writing. My iambic pentameter plays are a far cry from my modern work—and well they should be! As Sondheim says, "Content dictates form." What I'm writing alters how I write.

What do you hope to achieve with this work?
I hope that directors have a field day inventing new, practical solutions to the fantastical elements of the play. This really is a delightful play to work on, and a luminous play to produce. Everyone goes away laughing, crying—it moves you, Bob. Also, puppets are *fun*.

What were the biggest challenges involved in the writing of this play?
There were a few. George MacDonald has the luxury of writing at length, which means that he can—and does—includes several chapters about the Princess' childhood. Chapters which are not important to the plot, although they're a lot of fun. So the first challenge was sorting out where the

heart of the story lay, and cutting away everything else.

The second challenge came later in revisions. In 2017, I gathered together some terrific New York City actors to read and rehearse the play with my theatre company, just so I could get fresh eyes on the piece. What I discovered was that people wanted to know more about the Witch (blame it on ***Wicked***)—and that what people were really reacting to were the lines that I'd added which weren't in the original novel. In revisiting the play, then, I took a few more liberties with the text: sharpening the story to look at why the Witch was unsuitable to rule the land, as well as delving in deeper to the ramifications of the Princess only being able to laugh, even when she's terrified.

Finally, when I first wrote the play, I had almost no stage directions! That's the joy of writing a script that you know you're going to direct. After having played with the text for six months during the touring premiere, and then again with New York City actors, it was great fun to add in stage directions which, I hope, give the sense of those silent scenes and wonder that are important to the play.

What are the most common mistakes that occur in productions of your work?

There are two. As mentioned, I love it when companies take ownership of a play and make it amusing to their particular audience. To that end, I almost always add in little places where the producing company is welcome to make changes. Sometimes, companies don't take advantage of that, and the work doesn't sparkle quite as much. I encourage you to be inventive. The other common mistake is to approach the text too slow. I write *quick* dialogue. Even if there's a considerable amount of stage directions, keep the pace moving along. Even silent scenes should have a pace. It doesn't need to be frantic by any means, and of course there's going to be one or two moments of beautiful stillness, but for Heaven's sake, *don't plod.*

What inspired you to become a playwright?
I honestly didn't recognize that I was a playwright until I'd written and directed somewhere upward of 30 shows. My very first plays were in first and second grade, when I'd make my friends rehearse our make-believe, with myself taking the juiciest role and then narrating events. In third grade, I liked one of our pretends about two orphan sisters so much (I was a huge ***Annie*** and ***Oliver!*** fan, obviously), that I actually started writing sheet music for a sung-through musicalized version of the story! But I still didn't think I was a playwright. The story just needed music. Later, I'd write, direct, and star in one-acts that I'd write for camp counselors to perform. These, too, I didn't recognize as plays. I just refused to do their dumb skits and so offered to write something better. And so it goes, and so it goes.

In high school, I wrote an Oscar Wilde-lite one-act which eventually we put on in college—which confirmed my belief that I was a director, but not a playwright. While teaching high school, we were given no budget, so it was either Shakespeare or original work. I wrote a lot of stuff. But it wasn't until I published my first play while I was in grad school, receiving the contract to publish on a particularly hard day when I was trudging around Boston Common, that it struck me: Oh. I guess I have written a lot of plays. Oh. I guess I am a playwright.

Sometimes, being a little stupid can be useful. If you don't know you can't do something, then one day you look back and see that you've been achieving the impossible for quite a long time.

What is your writing process?
I like spring-boarding off of known structures, like fairy tales. However, when you're deepening mythology, the first question you have to ask is: "What is this story *about*?" "*Why* do I need to rewrite the end of *Cinderella*?" "What deeper truth am I trying to convey?" So first I choose the story form, then I look deeper into that form to its underlying philosophy. After that, I tend to name the characters I think might be in the play, and pinpoint the major tent-poles of action: beginning, middle, end. Then I start writing!

What frequently happens is that variations start to appear: characters I thought I'd need fall away; other ones pop up. And as I try to dig deeper and deeper into the philosophical question, I diverge further and further from the givens of the original story. That's the trickiest bit: because you want to be true to what the audience wants (for example, if you have *Cinderella,* there had better be a glass slipper!), but you also want to bring the audience where they didn't know they actually wanted to go.

Once a draft of the play is written—or often before I've finished—I call up my actor friends and ask them to come over and give the play a read. However, there have been many, many times when I don't have that luxury and just jump into rehearsals and fix the play as we go! The trick is to be true to what the story wants to be. I'm just the conduit, that's all. Theatre needs to be alive. My ego's not important.

Shakespeare gave advice to the players in *Hamlet;* if you could give advice to your cast what would it be?
Even if you think you're not the right "type" for the part, if you know your soul resonates with a role, audition for it! You are allowed to be on that stage. You are allowed to be an actor. You are allowed to spill your guts, no matter what your

outside looks like. (Your outside is beautiful, by the way. Don't let anyone tell you different.) Make mistakes! Have fun! Fail gloriously! Leave it on the stage, and take only the good parts back with you.

How was the first production different from the vision that you created in your mind?
The very first play I was aware that I was directing was ***The French Butler ~ An Evening's Diversion,*** which I wrote when I was in high school. I directed the show when I was a junior in college, and kept very true to my original ideas. As a result, the show was stagnant. People were kept in place. I barely made any bold decisions at all. My theatre professor came and saw the show, sat in the back and stroked his` beard. When it was over, he came up to me and all he said was: "Lopsided." Which was accurate. I had been so rigid, that the show was actually better viewed from one side of the house and not from the other.

I learned my lesson from that, and since then I've never written a play for a premiere that I was directing with many stage directions at all. I write the text and treat it like Shakespeare: something for myself, the cast, and crew to play with. So when I went into the first production for ***The Light Princess,*** I'd written perhaps a few ideas for myself ("Fabric for water? Hire extra men to keep the Princess aloft?"), but opened myself to every happy accident that rehearsal provides ("Platform with a hole in it? Prince can drown!"). I actually love seeing other productions of my work and how creative artistic minds can be. Hopefully, the suggestions (I mean, "stage directions") in ***The Light Princess*** can inspire you, too.

About the Author

Emily C. A. Snyder is a published and internationally produced playwright and novelist, whose work has been performed from Christchurch, New Zealand to Dublin, Ireland. A prolific writer and composer, she is the author of over 70 plays, musicals, operas, ballets, and masques. Her five-act iambic pentameter play, ***Cupid and Psyche ~ A New Play in Blank Verse,*** premiered in New York City to sold-out audiences. As a classical artist, she has directed the major works of Shakespeare's canon, and regularly teaches adults and adolescents about approaching his text. She has also had the pleasure of playing several of Shakespeare's most notable roles, including Rosalind from ***As You Like It*** in Stratford-upon-Avon, England, catty-corner from Shakespeare's birthplace. Snyder is the Co-Founder and Artistic Director of TURN TO FLESH PRODUCTIONS (TTF), a NYC-based theatre company specializing in new plays written in heightened styles featuring strong female protagonists. www.emilycasnyder.info.

About YouthPLAYS

YouthPLAYS was founded by playwrights and longtime friends Jonathan Dorf and Ed Shockley, who met in Philadelphia, where they ran the Philadelphia Dramatists Center. They were joined by Jonathan's friend from Harvard, playwright Matt Buchanan. YouthPLAYS started as a place for the trio to amplify their scripts for young actors and audiences. It has grown into a carefully curated catalogue of plays and musicals from over 200 playwrights. YouthPLAYS focuses on shows that center young people, from children to young adults, as well as plays of educational importance. At YouthPLAYS, we believe that theatre is hard enough without lots of red tape. We're here to make licensing easy. With one-business-day turnaround, responsive customer service, convenient digital scripts, copying and streaming options, we want to be your choice for challenging and entertaining shows, whether you're at a school, university or a theatre company.

About ProduceaPlay.com

Now that you've found a great script...let's put on a play! Producing a show can be lots of fun, but it takes hard work, knowledge, time and energy. While finding the time and energy (and maybe some coffee) is up to you, you're not in this alone. ProduceaPlay.com offers a wealth of knowledge and tips from theatre professionals for you to use. The site is completely free and organized to support your journey through the production process. Whether it's help meeting your licensing obligations, conducting auditions, publicizing performances or finding savvy solutions to any of the other creative challenges that come with mounting a show, this free resource can help make your production dreams a reality!

More from YouthPLAYS

A Nutcracker Story by Emily C. A. Snyder
Drama with music. 75-90 minutes. 6+ females, 3+ males, 1-15+ any (10-50+ performers possible).

Drawing from the Tchaikovsky ballet and E. T. A. Hoffman's original tale, ***A Nutcracker Story*** is part play, part musical, part ballet…and all magic. On Christmas Eve in 1812 Russia, Clara Silberhaus is one sleep away from entering adulthood. But with the last vestiges of war on the horizon, her father's life in danger and a rather irritating—and handsome—young prince come for the festivities, is growing up what Clara really wants? With a little help from her mysterious Uncle Drosselmeier, can Clara dance past her fears (and some troublesome rats) and into a land of newfound courage and a little holiday hope?

Jack in the Box by Scott Mullen
Horror. 25-30 minutes. 4 females, 1 male.

Four teenage girls at a slumber party are tempted by a voice from a box, which claims to be able to direct them to the future they want, if only they'll do what it says—and give it what it needs…

The Locker Next 2 Mine by Jonathan Dorf
Dramedy. 80-85 minutes. 8-16+ females, 5-12+ males (14-40 performers possible).

Alisa arrives at a new high school in the middle of the year to find her locker next to a shrine for a popular lacrosse player who's died in an auto accident, but as she digs deeper, she discovers another death that no one talks about, even as it's left many of the school's students trying to pick up their own pieces. A play about teen suicide and dealing with loss.

Jennifer the Unspecial: Time Travel, Love Potions & 8th Grade by Matthew Mezzacappa (book & lyrics) & Cynthia Chi-Wing Wong (music)
Musical. 90 minutes. 3-30 females, 5-30 males (8-60 performers possible).

When her science teacher's invention goes horribly wrong, awkward, clumsy eighth grader Jennifer finds herself thrust into a time-traveling adventure with three of her classmates. Through the journey, as they encounter warriors, artists, presidents and love potions, Jennifer discovers she doesn't need anyone's approval to be absolutely amazing and special.

Cinderella: The Fairy Godmother's Tale by Louise Keeton
Comedy for Young Audiences. 30-40 minutes. 3-5 females, 1-3 males (6 performers total).

Everyone knows what happened at the ball, but no one knows what the Fairy Godmother had to do for Cinderella to win the prince's heart. Follow Phoebe, the newest Fairy Godmother-in-Training as she learns that real magic comes from hard work and faith in yourself. It's the classic story we all know and love, but with lots of laughter and a surprising magical twist!

Dancing With Myself by Leanne Griffin
Dramedy. 35-45 minutes. 7 females.

Goth Girl. Moody Chick. Gamer. Cheerleader. New Kid. Jock. Nerd. Seven high school girls and the labels they've been forced to wear. But in this innovative, award-winning dramedy, whether it's sports or a sleepover or the classroom or a school dance or the ups and downs of daily life, they'll use music as their inspiration to break free of the stereotypes and discover the unique identity they each possess.